Practical Cybersecurity for Your Mom

Protecting yourself from attackers, attorneys, and assholes for the non-technical person

Michael P. Simone, CISSP and other certifications which are meaningless to non-industry people.

Copyright © 2017 by Michael P. Simone

All rights reserved. No part of this publication may be reproduced, distributed, or transmitted in any form or by any means, including photocopying, recording, or other electronic or mechanical methods, without the prior written permission of the publisher, except in the case of brief quotations embodied in critical reviews and certain other noncommercial uses permitted by copyright law.

Third Edition

Contents

Introduction 4
   Why should you listen to me? (A.K.A. About the Author) 4
   Style Consideration 6
Securing the Home Network 7
   Stop Letting Your Neighbors Use Your Wireless 14
   Stop Letting Your Network be Used Against You 16
Protecting your Online Identity 22
   Let's talk about browsers. 23
   One Ring to Rule Them All 25
Securing Your Endpoints 34
   Basic System Readiness 36
   Malware and Antivirus 45
   Back dat ass up! 52
   Keeping the Bad Guys Away 53
Final Thoughts 59
Appendix A: Firewall Ports and Protocols 60
Glossary 62

Introduction

Hardly a day goes by that one of my friends doesn't ask me about how to protect their machines at home. Either they ask me directly, or they post some sort of question to their Facebook page, and hope that I see the waves of well-meaning idiots wading in with erroneous and apocryphal advice that will only lead them into trouble. So, because I'm genuinely concerned about making sure that people browse the Internet safely, I've decided to write the definitive guide to securing your home network for people who don't know anything about computers. **Everything I'm suggesting here is free.** Some of the items offer additional, premium services for a fee, but what I'm describing is the free stuff.

Throughout this note, I'm going to use some terms you might find scary, there's a Glossary at the back.

Why should you listen to me? (A.K.A. About the Author)

That's a good question, Gentle Reader. Why *should* you listen to me? After all, I have a wife, two kids, and four dogs, and none of them listen to me, so what makes this different? Well, I'll tell you.

I've been in the Information Security business for the last 17 years. I've worked in security operations centers (SOC's), I've designed and deployed network security systems for Fortune 500 companies, and I've spent the last four years completely focused solely on deploying anti-malware systems for my company's customers. I've spent countless hours doing incident response, firewall configuration, intrusion detection and prevention system maintenance, security policy design, auditing, and, basically, everything but penetration testing (sometimes called "ethical hacking"). I haven't been a pen-tester because I have focused so hard on defense that I don't know how to play offense. To your benefit, however, the knowledge and skills for which I get pimped out for hundreds of dollars per hour are yours for just reading this guide, and actually implementing what I show you.

Style Consideration

There will be times that, to explain something, I actually do need to get technical. I preface these with a "Nerd Alert", and then put the text in a different font, like this:

This is an example of technical stuff. If you don't care why something works, or why it's important, but just want to use it, you can skip over anything in this format.

That way, you don't have to worry about getting bored by technical details, while still being able to reap the benefits.

Securing the Home Network

Let's start with the network. Why? Well, considering what is probably in your home, that's the easiest place to begin. First things first. How is your home connected to the Internet? Either your cable or DSL provider has given you some sort of router. (If you're still using dial-up, well, by the time you finish downloading this guide, they'll have broadband in your neighborhood, so, good luck with that.) *Hopefully*, it's separate from your Wireless Access Point (WAP). It usually is. So, we want to start with your WAP, because you definitely do not want to screw with your router without your Internet Service Provider (ISP) telling you what to do. If they are not separate, you will need to call your ISP and ask them to make these changes for you.

Your WAP is probably made by either DLink or Netgear. There's documentation (Google is your friend) for exactly how to configure whatever model number it says on the [back/bottom] of your device. Here, I'll show some configuration guides from the most common WAPs I see in peoples' homes. If yours is not represented here, you'll need to find your WAP maker's website, and download the manual from there.

To get to the configuration of them, I have to go to the Internet address that was assigned to that device from my web browser. So, the first step is to find out what the IP address of your WAP is. You'll do that by opening a command prompt. On Windows 10, that's handled by right-clicking the Windows icon in the lower-left corner of your screen, and selecting Command Prompt. (Your machine might have been configured to use Powershell, like mine. Either one will work.)

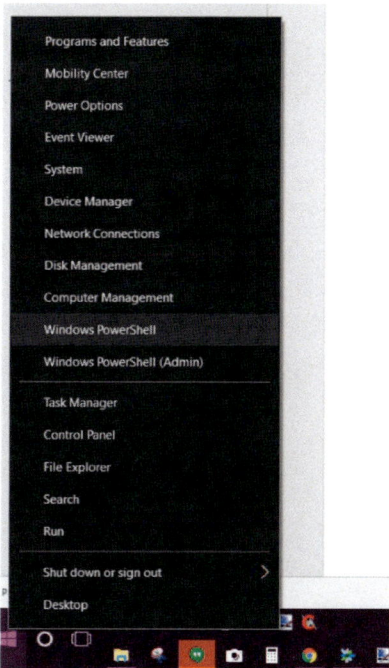

This will pop up a command window, which will look like this:

Pretty, right? Now, type `ipconfig` and press enter:

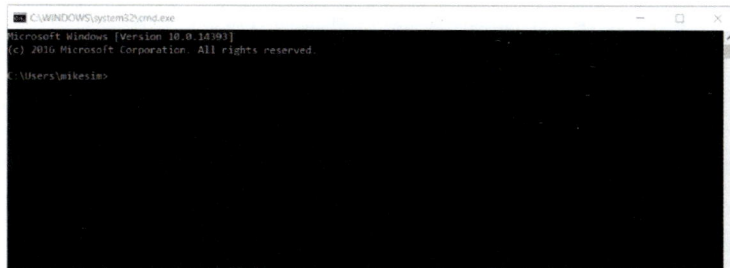

You may show multiple different adapters. Right now, I'll only care about the one that is connected to your WiFi. Write down the address listed by "Default Gateway". Mine is 192.168.0.1. Yours may be 192.168.1.1, but it probably won't be anything wildly different from either of those, unless whoever set up your network for you thinks they're clever. From there, you can proceed onward to [D-Link](#) or [Netgear](#) to configure your device.

D-Link

D-Link makes good, cheap, network gear, like [switches](#) and WAP's. I have a bunch of them scattered around my house. To access the configuration, I will open a browser to https://192.168.0.1 (the address from my listing of my default gateway from above.) It will complain about not being secure. Ignore the warning and proceed. You'll be presented with a login page. The default password for a D-Link WAP is usually not set, so admin as the username and a blank will *probably* get you in. Yes, the first thing you need to do is set a password for administration.

You change that by going to the "Tools" tab, and then selecting the Admin menu. Set a password and click "Save". Probably a good idea to keep that password in mind; you'll need it for a later section of the guide.

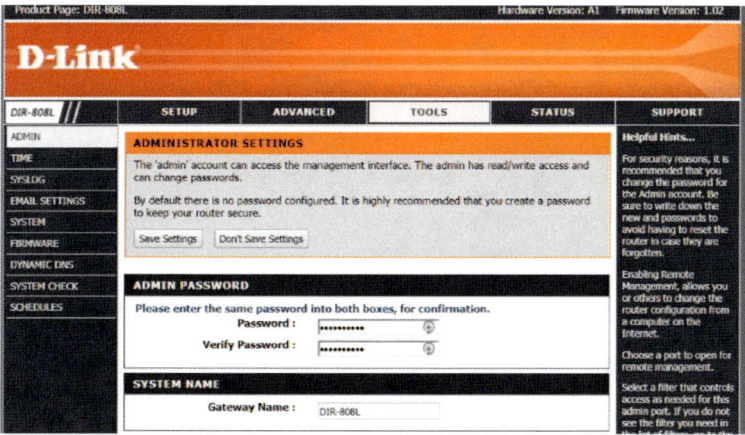

Once you've done that, click "Setup", then "Wireless Settings", then "Manual Wireless Setup". (See image on next page.)

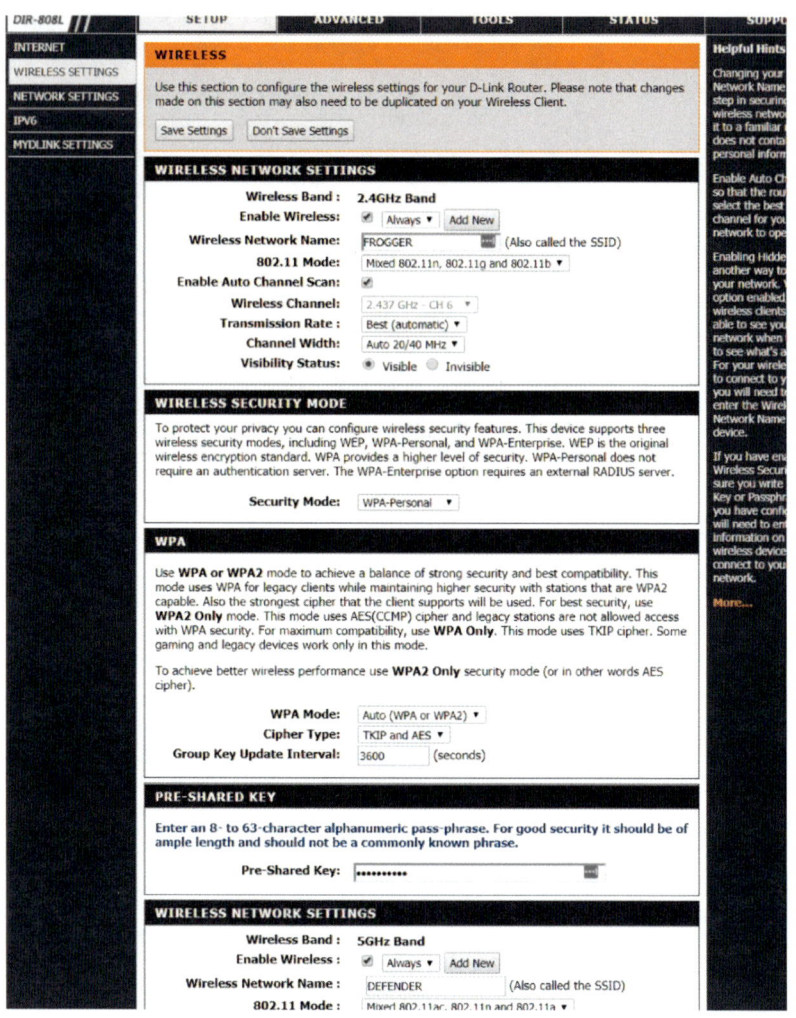

From there, you can continue to the next section.

Netgear

Netgear makes some of the most ubiquitous network gear on the planet. They're everywhere. One of the cool features of them is that you can erase the "brain" of them and put in your own firmware, called DD-WRT, and use that, instead. I will **not** be showing how to use DD-WRT, because the types of nerd who can install that already know all these settings tricks, anyway.

Just like with the D-Link, you'll want to open your browser to http://192.168.0.1 (unless your default gateway was different), and log in. The default password is "password", so try that. If you can get in, you'll also want to change that password. Go to the Wireless Settings Menu, and then continue on with the next section. (Screenshot from their manual.)

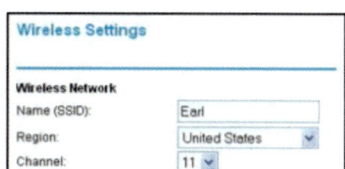

Figure 3-4: Wireless Settings menu

Stop Letting Your Neighbors Use Your Wireless

This one is easy. You probably left your SSID (that's the name that gets broadcast out so you know which wireless network to which to connect) as the default. If I look in my neighborhood, I see four default router names, and a printer.

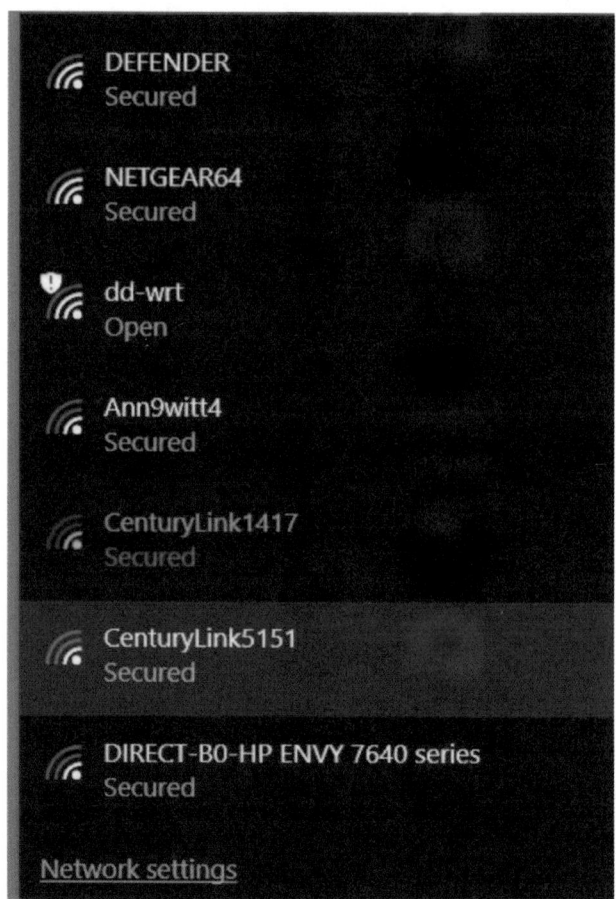

And one neighbor who tried to do it right, but ... no.

The first thing you need to do is make sure that you set an SSID that you can remember, but that doesn't contain the security key in it. For example, every WAP in my house is named after a 1980's video game. I have

Frogger, Defender, Pac-Man, Dig-Dug, Centipede – you get the gist.

This next part is **VERY IMPORTANT**: You MUST set up wireless security on it. **DO NOT USE WEP**. WEP can be cracked in minutes. In the dropdown menu, use WPA-2. It'll ask if you want to use a pre-shared key (PSK) or 802.1x. Since you *probably* don't have any sort of directory services or identity and access management services running in your house, select PSK. Select something easy for you to remember, but hard to guess, like `Ilike2RunNakedInMyYardAtNight$`. You're not going to type it very often, so that would be fine. Use something that means something to you.

Why would we do this? Because it keeps people from, innocently or not, using your WiFi. You're the one paying for your Internet connection; you may as well get to use all the bandwidth for *your* Netflix streaming. But, far more importantly, people can get up to some nasty things if they have access to your network. They can impersonate a device on your network, and intercept your network traffic, to steal your passwords or data. (A process called a "man-in-the-middle" attack.) Nefarious people could connect to your network from their car out on the street, and use it to attack companies or governments. They might use it to download child pornography. When the FBI kicks in your door and hauls you off to jail, they won't believe that you weren't the one using your network to do nasty things.

Stop Letting Your Network be Used Against You

The next step is creating an environment that is hostile to attackers. The first step towards that is to make sure that you render as many of their tools inoperable as possible.

Operator, How May I Help You?

We start by making sure that your computers are less likely to be able to communicate with the attackers. We do that by protecting your DNS hygiene. Of course, we need to know what that means, right? So, what is DNS, and why is it important?

Every machine on the Internet has an address, and that address is represented by a number. (It's a 32-bit binary number, usually written as xxx.xxx.xxx.xxx.) Of course, nobody can remember all of those numbers and what they mean, so, like the old Yellow Pages (remember those?), the Domain Name System (DNS) is a directory of all of those numbers sorted by

friendly names. So, instead of going to 8.8.8.8, you go to Google.com. OpenDNS Umbrella uses very complicated systems to determine if a particular domain name (like kasunguzxuhf.com) is legit or malicious, and, if it's malicious, will return a safe address and a page telling you that you tried to go to a malware domain, and to stop that. 93% of all malware uses DNS to identify and connect to its command and control channels (C2), so, by using OpenDNS, you take care of 93% of the malware problem right off the bat.

Go to https://signup.opendns.com/homefree and create an account. This will give you the ability to use OpenDNS Umbrella (consumer version) to protect your entire network. For home users, this is free. (It costs money for businesses.) Home users also get some limited filtering capabilities, so you can impede your kids' attempts to look at porn. (Just remember, if you block Ashley Madison and your spouse suddenly becomes grumpy, don't blame me.) Once you've signed up, you'll be presented with a setup screen. When you click "Home Router", it will take you to the OpenDNS help site, which will contain the easy-to-follow setup instructions for about every router available on the market to make sure that you're providing the right DNS servers to all of your home systems.

Now that your network will be using OpenDNS to protect you, you need to add your IP addresses for protection. Go to http://www.ipchicken.com, and write down the IP address it shows you.

Now, add that in the OpenDNS page:

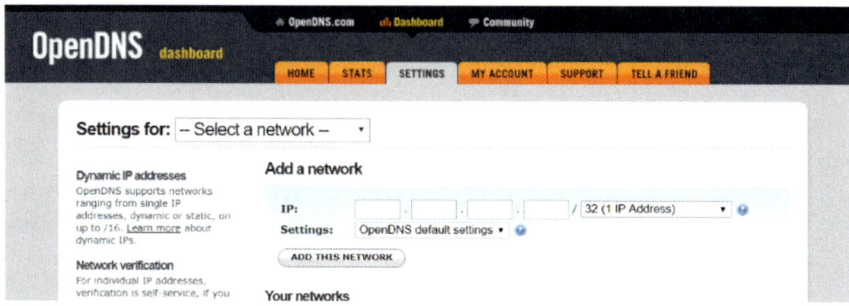

If it successfully adds (and it should), you can now click on that IP address, and manage settings for those machines.

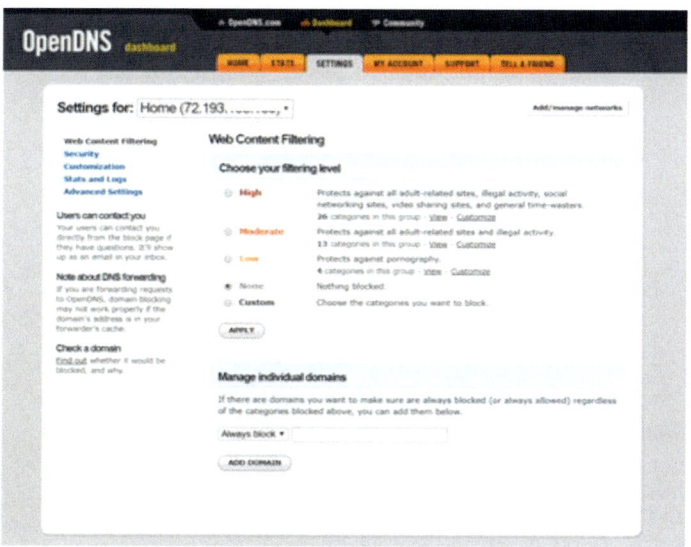

Click "Custom" and select what you want to block. This will allow you to filter things like keeping your kids from browsing porn, etc.

FIRE! (Enabling Firewall Services)

*Turn on the basic firewall system that is in your WAP. (There should be a tab for it, and it's in the instructions.) If you're feeling REALLY adventurous, you can set up <u>egress filtering</u>, but the benefits to that are minimal these days. If you're not feeling adventurous, go ahead and skip on to <u>**Securing Your Online Identity**</u> or <u>**Securing the Endpoint**</u>. That said, if you **really** want to lock your network down to only those things that you think you'll need, please see Appendix A for a list of ports and protocols you would want to enable.*

By default, the firewall should be enabled in the WAP. If it is not, make sure your settings match this:

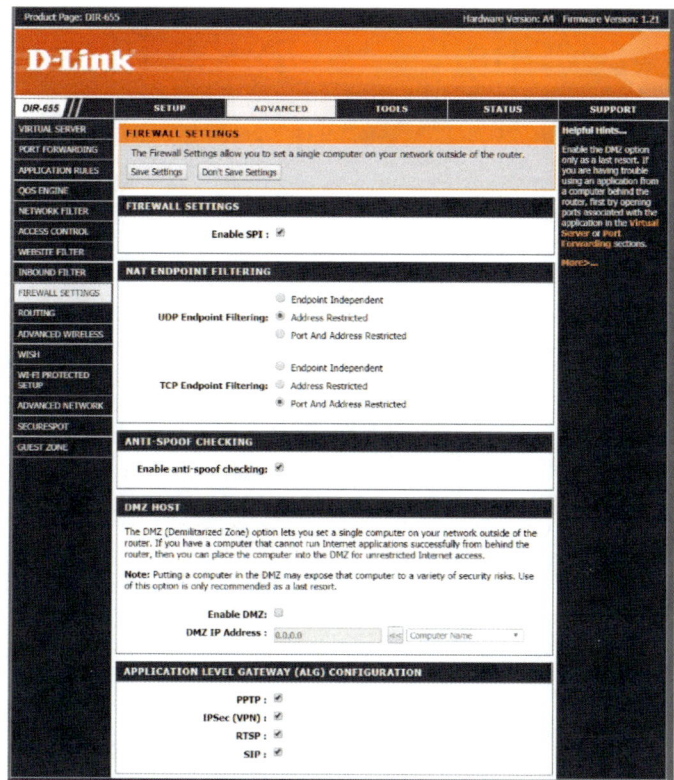

These will help prevent attackers from being able to access your machine from the outside.

Protecting your Online Identity

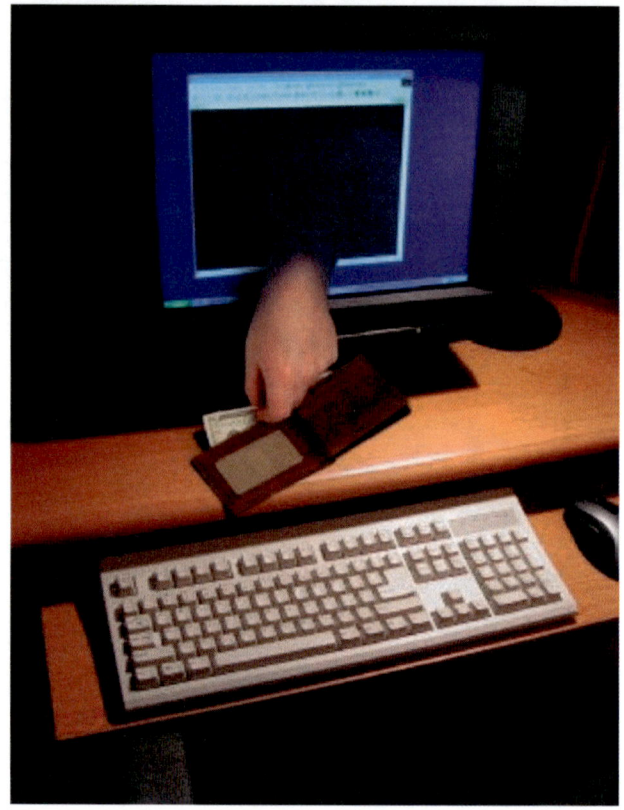

Let's talk about browsers.

Stop hitting yourself! Stop hitting yourself!

Are you using Internet Explorer or Microsoft Edge? **STOP IT**.

Go download Chrome right now. https://www.google.com/chrome/browser/

Install that, make it your default browser, and use it. You'll need it for the later tools, anyway. Delete the Internet Explorer and Edge icons from your desktop, your start menu, your quick launch bar, and anywhere else you have them. You could also use Firefox, but I find it painfully resource intensive, so I use Chrome.

Reducing Eye Strain and Ass-ache

One of the big features of Chrome is the ability to use extensions. One of the extensions I find to be most helpful for security is uBlock Origin. It blocks ads on pages, and it's fantastic. https://www.ublock.org/ Now, why would I have an ad-blocker in a post about security? Malicious ads – malvertisments.

On the Internet, things can look just fine, and still be really bad for you. For example, if I'm an attacker, and I buy an ad on your favorite news station's web site, and then that ad has a hidden 1x1-pixel graphic within it which, in the background, pulls down my malicious content on your machine, you're suddenly hosed. The ad blocker prevents that. You may think that it's porn sites which are getting your computer sick, but it's really the ads on legitimate sites. Porn sites depend heavily on people visiting them repeatedly, so they actually work a lot harder to prevent giving you malware than "reputable" sites.

One Ring to Rule Them All

I bet you have one password that you use on every site. Sure, on some sites, you add a number or an exclamation point. Sometimes you capitalize the first letter. If you've ever wondered why it's such a bad thing with all the passwords for one site get dumped, it's because, like you, most people use several variants of that one password. This is one of the worst things you can do to yourself online. (It ranks somewhere between sexting your boss and posting Instagram photos of your credit cards.) XKCD created a wonderful cartoon on password creation:

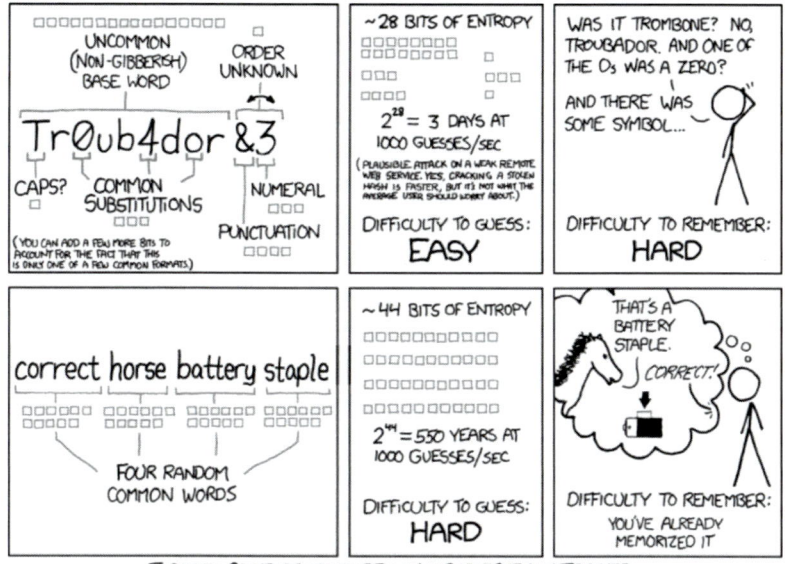

You need a password manager. There are many out there, but my favorite is LastPass. I like it because it syncs across multiple devices (such as my work and personal laptops, plus my phone and tablet); it never stores the [encryption / decryption key](#) anywhere, so, even if they get hacked, you're safe; and I just really like the interface. It can be acquired at https://lastpass.com/f?5424006, and it is free. If you want the ability to sync to multiple devices including mobile, and to share certain passwords with the rest of your family, it's a whopping $24[1] / year. Probably won't break you.

On the LastPass site, create an account. The first step will be creating a passphrase for your password vault. **Since this is the only one you will need to memorize,** I suggest a passphrase. (But, please, do *not* use, "Correct Horse Battery Staple".) It should include a mix of upper- and lower-case, symbols, and numbers. It can take special characters, but, be forewarned, any special character you can't recreate on your phone will be a problem for you when you try to use it on mobile. (So, no alt-codes.) Some people like to use a song lyric, or a favorite passage from a book. "If I did have a tumor, I'd name it Marla." would be nearly impossible for a computer to crack. It should include a mix of upper- and lower-case, symbols, and numbers. It can take special characters, but, be forewarned, any special character you can't recreate on your phone will be a problem for you when you try to use it on mobile. (So, no alt-codes.)

Download and install the Chrome browser extension, and let it import all of your saved passwords. (Yes, I know you told it to save that easy password for every site because you hate typing it.) Don't be embarrassed. This is how you learn. Once they're all imported, then open your LastPass vault and run the Security Challenge.

---

[1] Literally the *day* after the first edition came out, they raised their prices, so older versions have $12.

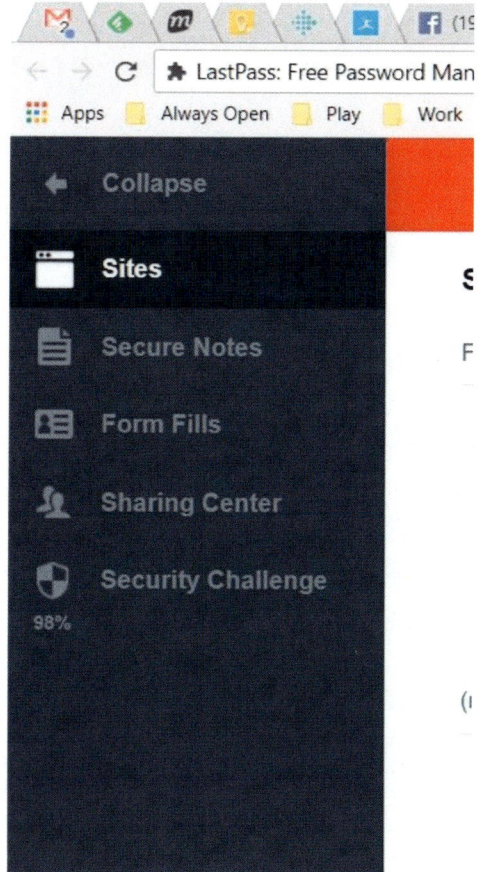

This will be time consuming to do right, but *so very worth the effort.*

- It will make sure that you aren't using the same password on multiple sites.
- It'll make sure you're not using weak passwords.
- It'll make sure you're not using old passwords

    Just follow the prompts. For some sites, it can change the password for you. On others, you must do it manually.

Your first time through, you won't have any old passwords to change.

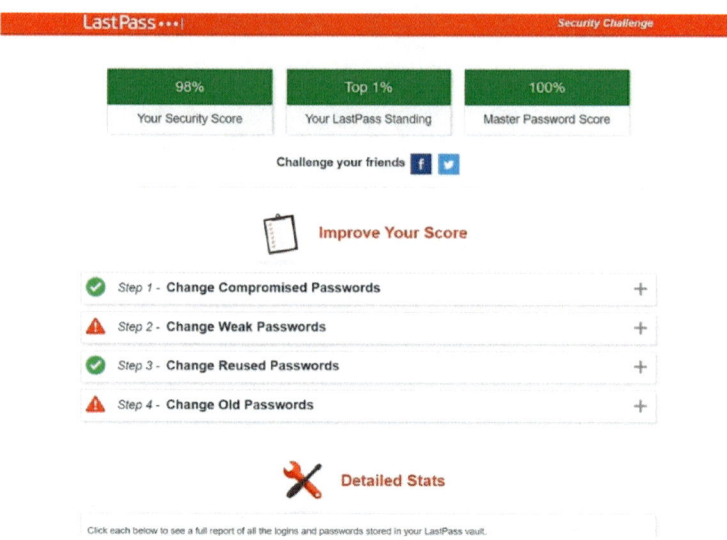

You see how I've got a 98% on there? That's because I have one site that won't let me put in a complex password (morons), and a ton that are old. About once per month, I go through, and I spend time trying to update all of the old passwords. I have hundreds of sites for which to do this, so I am always running behind. It takes a long time, because most sites make the "change password" part impossible to find. I'll never be at 100%, because some sites simply will not let you change your password, ever, because they're horrible.

I also use the form fills in LastPass, too. That way, when I buy stuff online, it can fill in all my credit card info automatically. (Don't worry, it's only saved encrypted, with the strongest commercially-available encryption algorithm on the market, and the only person who knows the key is you.) That keeps me from having to save my credit card information on multiple sites who might get compromised. I retain the data, not them. Why does Domino's Pizza need to keep my credit card information, when I can have my browser extension fill it all when I want to order some delicious pizza? This one step can save you hundreds of hours of dealing with fraud prevention departments.

But what if I die? How will my spouse log into our banking and insurance sites?

Everyone in your family should be using LastPass, and you can share passwords easily that way by clicking the "share" button. With that, you can list a designated recovery agent. They will gain access a certain number of hours after a request unless you stop them. That way, if you are dead, your designated recovery agent can access your sites.

1. Open your LastPass Vault
2. Click on the life ring icon in the lower left

3. Click the plus sign in the lower right. Add in the email of someone you trust, like a spouse, and set the waiting period time (default is 48 hours).
4. Once they accept, they'll show up under people you trust.

Now, since you installed Chrome, and you installed the Lastpass Chrome extension, it'll fill in those new, automatically generated passwords for you. Make sure you always use it to create a new password for every site. Use the maximum length password for each site, and let it generate them for you.

Let it do the thinking for you. You still only need to remember one password, but a hacker getting your Facebook password won't get into your bank account.

Sweet. Now, nobody can ever pretend to be me.

Not so fast, there, cowboy. The next phase is called two-factor authentication (2FA). "What is that?" It means that you have two separate pieces of information to log in. The general rule is authentication can be granted by something you know (password), something you have (token, certificate), or something you are (biometrics), and having two or more to log in is a good thing. Thus, your next stop is http://www.authy.com/. Create an account (***DO NOT USE THE SAME PASSWORD FOR AUTHY AND LASTPASS***) install it in Chrome and on your phone, and then consult this list: https://twofactorauth.org/

There are myriad 2FA programs out there. Why Authy? Because I'm forgetful and lazy. You probably are, too, so listen up. Authy will synchronize that token across your phone, your tablet, and your browser extension. It can automatically copy the code into your clipboard and paste it into the prompt so that you don't even have to remember six digits for five seconds to type them in to the browser yourself. Even more importantly, have you ever, on a whim, gone to your cellular provider and swapped out your phone for some newer, shinier, faster, prettier model only to get home and you realize you forgot to transfer some stuff over? Yeah, me, too. Authy prevents you from doing that with the token generator that will control access to everything in your life.

Log into every site you frequent, and turn on two-factor authentication. MOST of the time, they'll just have a barcode you scan with Authy on your phone, and, every sixty seconds, a new, second password that you have to enter when you log on will appear in the Authy app on your phone. That way, even if someone DOES get your password, it doesn't do them any good unless they also compromise Authy. Now, some sites don't let you use your own authentication token. Some of them will only text you a code to input, or email it, or do some other nonsense instead of just letting you use your token. (Looking at you, PayPal.)

So, where should I use 2FA? **Everywhere.** But start with:

- Your email account. Google, Yahoo, all of them offer 2FA options. If people can't get to your email, they will have a harder time doing the password recovery thing to get your password. Authy even includes set-up guides on their site for how to configure all the major websites to use them. Here's the one for Gmail: https://authy.com/guides/gmail/
- Your bank accounts.
- Your credit card accounts.

- Amazon, eBay, PayPal - anywhere you spend money often.

Securing Your Endpoints

There are many pieces to this; I know it's going to seem overwhelming at first. Just remember, though, I'm only listing things that require zero or minimal configuration. I want making your home system secure to be an easy, painless, quick thing, that you set and forget. But, now I need to talk to you a bit about the big, bad world, malware, and the absolutely useless antivirus that you're already running on your PC.

Basic System Readiness

They say the journey of a thousand miles begins with a leaky tire and a faulty fuel pump. Just like you would probably never buy a $300 jalopy and take it on a cruise from coast to coast without an overhaul, you also want to perform regular system maintenance on your PC. The most basic of these system maintenance requirements is patching your software. The best place to start with that is patching your system. Patches should be installed automatically as soon as they come out, so that your machine is always secured against the most recent vulnerabilities.

1. In Windows 10, Click "Start", then click the "Settings" button on the right side of the menu. It looks like a cog in the lower left.

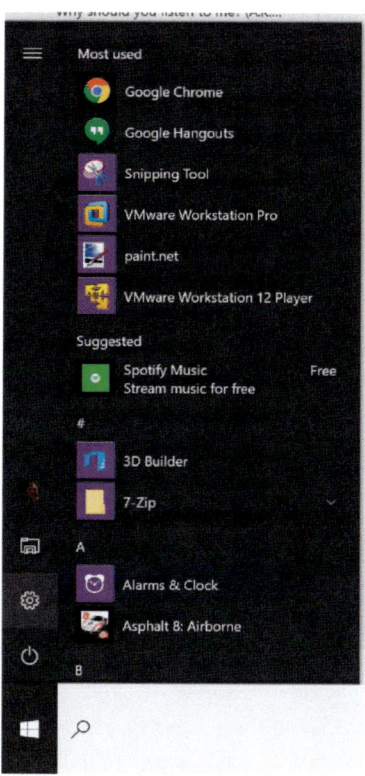

2. Click "Update and Security"

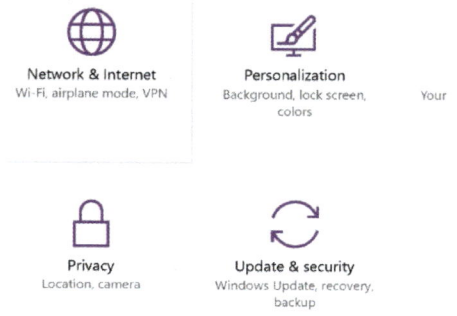

3. Select "Advanced Options"

> Update settings
>
> Available updates will be downloaded and installed automatically, except over metered connections (where charges may apply).
>
> Change active hours
>
> Restart options
>
> Advanced options
>
> Looking for info on the latest updates?
> Learn more

4. Enable updates for other Microsoft products during updates

> Choose how updates are installed
>
> ☑ Give me updates for other Microsoft products when I update Windows.
>
> ☐ Defer feature updates
> Learn more
>
> ☐ Use my sign in info to automatically finish setting up my device after an update.
> Learn more
>
> Privacy statement
>
> Choose how updates are delivered
>
> Note: Windows Update might update itself automatically first when checking for other updates.
>
> Privacy settings

5. Close the "Settings" window.

Now, this will update your Microsoft Windows and Office products, but what about all of the other things you use? Follow some simple rules:

- If any of your software has options for automatic updates, select it.
- If any of your software prompts you to update it, update it.

- If you're not getting prompted by that software for regular security updates, find an alternative to it that *does* get regular updates.

For example, with Google Chrome:

1) If you see this little green arrow over the settings menu, Chrome wants to update. Click it, and Chrome will automatically update and restart.

2) If you don't trust it to update, you can check manually.
3) Click the settings menu in the upper right. (It has three dots.)

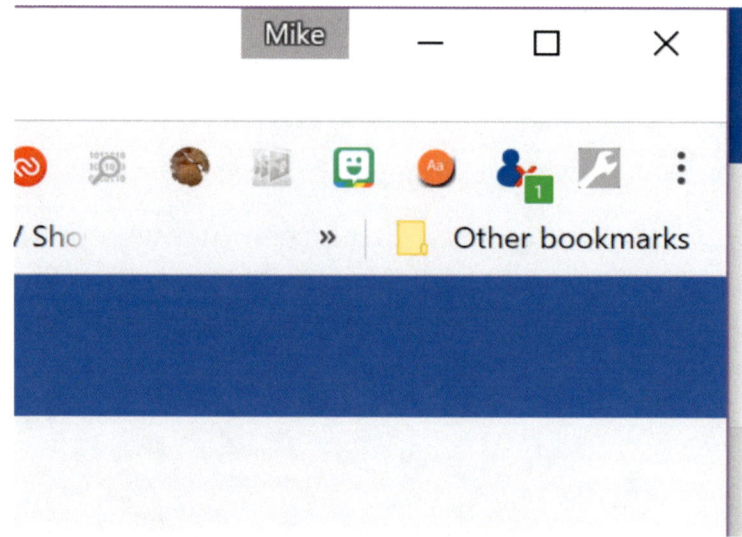

4) Click "Help"
5) Click "About Chrome"
6) If it needs an update, it will tell you. It will normally say "Up-to-date"

All software has vulnerabilities. There's no way around it. Software is too complex and intricate to find all of the vulnerabilities before it gets published, so make sure you keep up with your patches. If you are curious about what vulnerabilities are on your system, there is a free tool by Flexera to scan your machine and tell you which updates you need.

http://learn.flexerasoftware.com/SVM-EVAL-Personal-Software-Inspector

1. Download the software from the link above, and run it.
2. Select a language.
3. Keep the default

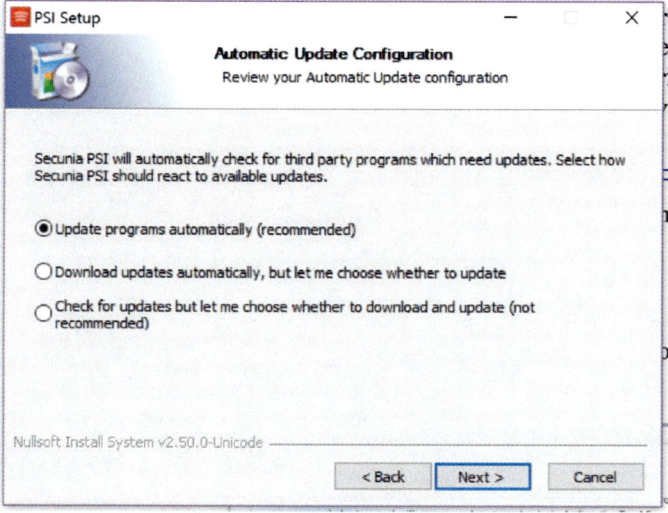

4. Say Yes

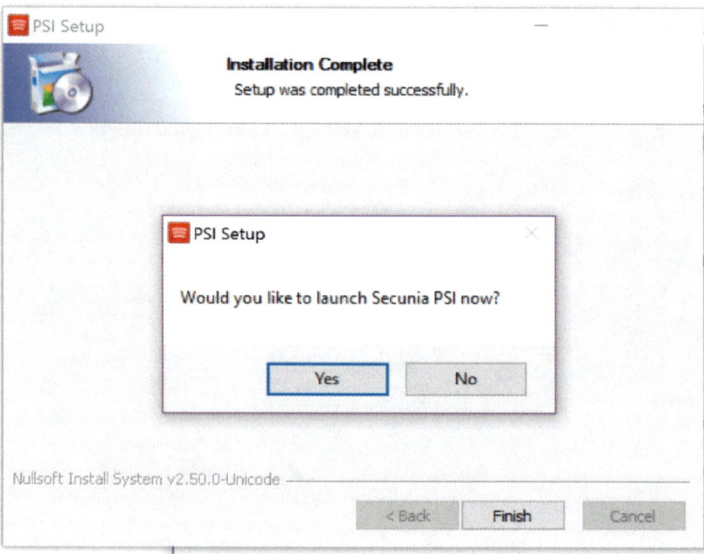

5. Run a scan

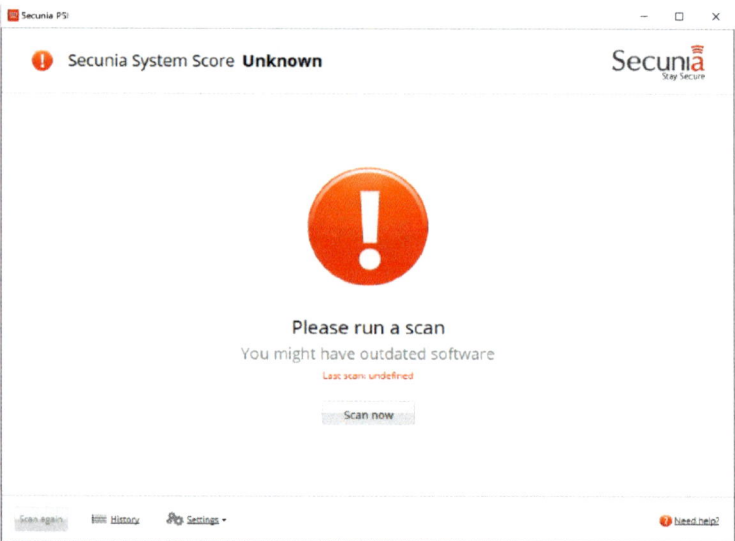

6. Follow any recommended updates

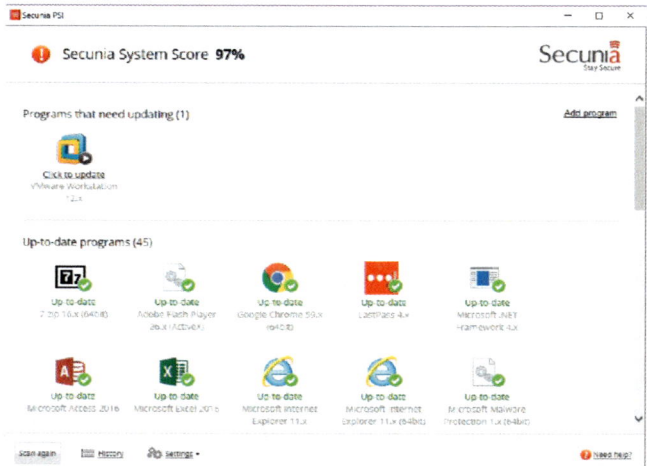

7. Make sure it remains set to update in the background

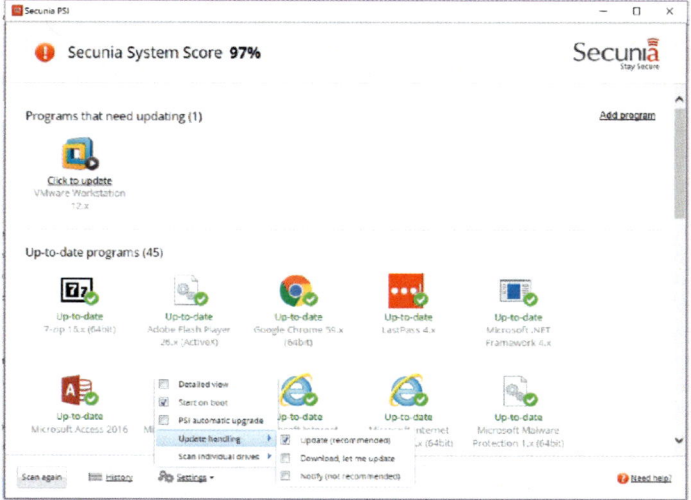

Now, your PC will remain updated.

You can also do the Qualys Browser Check: https://browsercheck.qualys.com/ . Just click "Scan Now", and it'll find and fix your vulnerabilities in your browser and extensions.

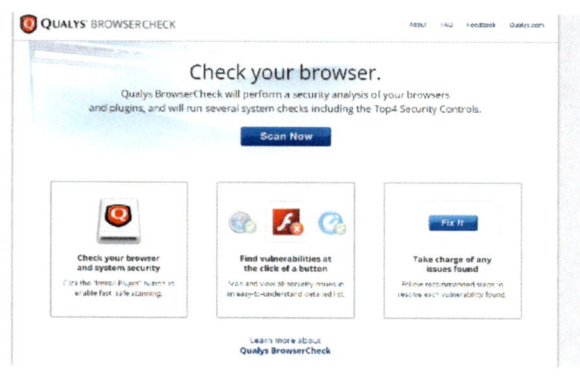

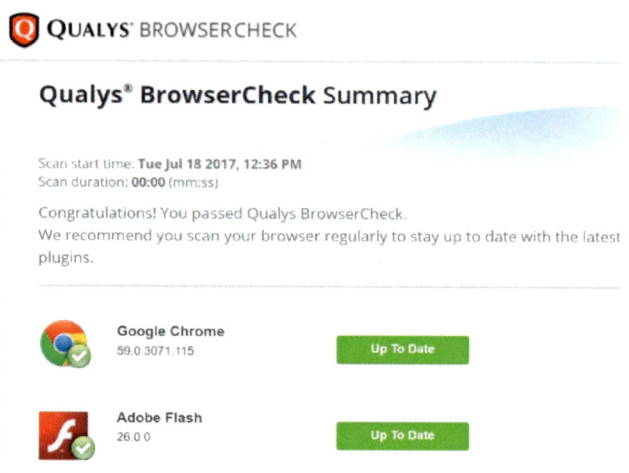

Surprise, I passed.

Malware and Antivirus

Think of the Internet as the busiest, cheapest prostitute in Thailand. Signature-based Antivirus is like picking up a used condom from her trash can, turning it inside out, and wearing that while you transact business with her. It not only provides you no protection, but it actually makes things worse because people who don't understand how viruses get transmitted will actually think they are protected. See, right up until you read that sentence, you probably thought your McAfee, or Norton, or AVG, or Vipre, or any of the other garbage that came preinstalled on your PC was actually helping you. Or maybe you thought you were clever, and put Kaspersky, or Avast, or some other thing that you downloaded thinking that, because it's obscure, the malware authors are unfamiliar with it. So, bad news, you're probably already infected, you just don't know it.

All traditional antivirus uses something called signatures. You've probably heard about "updating your antivirus signatures". What's a signature? A signature is a cryptographic output from a one-way algorithm which takes a variable-length input (i.e., it could be a simple text file that says, "Hello!", a copy of "War and

Peace", a program, a video, etc.), and returns a fixed-length, **unique** output. This output is called a "hash". There's many different types of hash. Most companies use SHA-256 (if it's a reputable company; if they're using MD5, they're **worse** than garbage) hash of a code sample, and compares it to a database of hashes. If it's in the database, then the antivirus (AV) quarantines the code. If not, it gets to run. The problem is that modern malware is polymorphic. (Greek for "many shapes".) Modern malware is often "reshaped" by doing simple things, like adding a null, or repacking with MPRESS, mfsvenom, UPX, etc. Doing multiple of those things makes it even more obfuscated. Due to that, signature-based antivirus is worthless. The average AV vendor, like McAfee, Symantec, Trend, Sophos, etc - they have about 20 million signatures. Sounds like a lot, right? My company is tracking over 150 million known malware families, each with their own polymorphic variants. So, that's about like betting all of your personal data on one number on the roulette wheel - and then hoping that bet pays of a few thousand times per day. You're going to lose, and lose badly.

So, what to do? Enter Immunet - or the commercial version, with enterprise-level management interfaces, AMP. It also starts (but ONLY starts) by filtering stuff out with a SHA-256. If it already knows about the file, it reacts accordingly. The next thing it does is process the attributes of the file through a machine learning algorithm and performs a Bayesian statistical analysis of the code sample to see if there's enough in common with existing malware to process a conviction. That's the second filter. That gets rid of a lot of low-hanging fruit. The next step is it goes to dynamic analysis - lets the code run, tracks changes to the file system, registry, mutexes, network calls, system calls, etc. If enough of those match indicators of compromise (IoC's), then it will go ahead and quarantine it. The next step is performing a fuzzy-fingerprinting type of de-obfuscation: things like looking for the decrypt algorithm for an encrypted payload, or looking for the hallmarks of a packer, etc. There's a few hundred different checks it runs. That's the last of the filtering. (Now, in reality, all these things are happening at the same time, but I like using words like "first" and "next".)

Then comes the meat. While it did the dynamic analysis in a sandbox, it does the real analysis on the end machine. Why? Because modern malware is often sandbox-aware. It looks for things like the number of document files on a machine, or a growing delta between the hardware clock and the system clock (or an NTP server.) It looks for particular user inputs, and reacts accordingly. Malware writers are intelligent, and they create new evasion techniques to counter our anti-evasion techniques every day. (My very favorite is Rombertik, which writes 100,000,000 random bytes to memory, each one requires its own line in the output log, which rapidly makes the log grow to several terabytes. Since that takes several minutes, it effectively works as a timer. Then it fires off some code to crash the debugger on the system, and, when it sees that crash, erases the master boot record and reboots the machine.) Immunet will watch for things like "Hey - why is Word calling Powershell?" or, "Hey, why is Acrobat Reader writing an executable?" or any of tens of thousands of other IoC's. Using that, it can take a previously unknown file, surface the threat, and eradicate it. It will also be able to show an analyst the other files which were created (since the initial dropper will put down keyloggers, rootkits, persistence mechanisms, information harvesters, etc.), so that those can be excised as well. Since it doesn't rely on on-box signatures, it's always up-to-date, and doesn't rely on signature updates. (And a lot of malware these days immediately edits your hosts file to redirect all of the AV update servers to 127.0.0.1, anyway, so you won't be able to push out signature updates anyway.)

So, you either skimmed or skipped the last few paragraphs, and said, "Mike does this for a living, so I'm gonna trust that he knows what he's talking about. Just tell me what to do." Now, it's *very important* that you do this in *this* order, or you could harm yourself.

1. Go to http://www.immunet.com/ and install Immunet. (Download, install, next your way through, click finish, celebrate giving future you the easiest free gift you've ever gotten.)

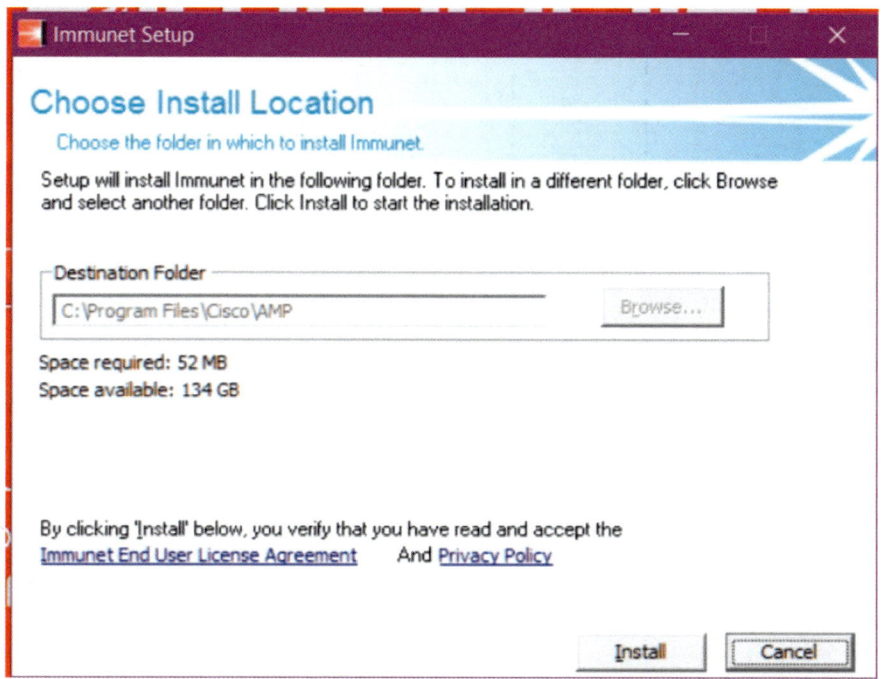

Gee, I wonder who makes Immunet.

2. Uninstall the garbage that came preinstalled on your computer. (Programs and Features, select your junk AV, click uninstall.)

3. Reboot to finish uninstalling the old stuff.

Between OpenDNS and Immunet, you've pretty much got the malware problem licked. Now, it's time to make sure that one bad day doesn't ruin your whole life.

But, Mike! I use a Mac, so I'm immune to malware.

HAHAHAHAHAHAHAHAHAHAHAHAHAHA HA They say God must love idiots, because he made so many of them. Apple's hype machine did a great disservice to the world, and left a gaping threat vector open to every graphic designer and effete "author" sitting in a Starbucks in the world. There are more real, exiled Nigerian princes trying to give you money in the world than there are computers which are immune to malware, and there are no royals trying to give you money. So, if you're using a Mac, at the ***very least***, install ClamAV from https://www.clamxav.com/ . It's not free, but, since you're using a Mac, you are clearly not hurting for money.

Back dat ass up!

Set up backups on your data. Set up backups in MULTIPLE PLACES! I back up to

- Google Backup (https://www.blog.google/products/photos/introducing-backup-and-sync-google-photos-and-google-drive/)
- Box.com (http://www.box.com)
- Dropbox.com (http://www.dropbox.com).
- OneDrive (https://onedrive.live.com/about/en-us/)

Why do I back up to that many places? Because I don't want one catastrophic event to hose my entire world. One gets compromised? I'm covered. I get hit with ransomware? The sync to at least one of them will come late enough that I can recover. Some of them even offer fallback to previous revisions. All of those are free for a certain amount of space. You can buy more if you need. The instructions for downloading and installing the sync package are on each site, so I will let you run with those. (And, of course, you're going to turn on 2FA for each of them, right?)

Lastly, it doesn't hurt to back up to some sort of external drive, local to your machine, too.

Keeping the Bad Guys Away

So, you've protected your online identity. You've stopped malware dead in its tracks. Everything looks good. Now, it's time to leave your house. Step one: Install the OpenDNS app for your iPhone, or DNS Changer for Android. https://play.google.com/store/apps/details?id=com.burakgon.dnschanger . It'll let you use OpenDNS when you connect to your 3/4G or WiFi hotspots. Yay! Install really any Android-based AV, too, and LastPass on your phones. If you have iPhone, you get no anti-malware protection, because Apple believes their own hype.

You grab your trusty laptop - but ***wait***! What if someone steals it? I mean, sure, you put a strong password on it to unlock it, or you're using the Windows Hello facial recognition (don't do that, since the government doesn't require a warrant to make you face your computer), but what if they run a password cracker on it? What if they just pull the hard drive out, and plug it into another machine as a secondary drive, and get at all of your delicious data! *Oh, NOEZ!*

Encrypt your hard drive with VeraCrypt. Some people recommend Bitlocker. Bitlocker replicates your decryption key up to Microsoft's sites so the FBI can decrypt your data. I don't care if you do or don't have something to hide, it's none of their business either way without a warrant. So, use VeraCrypt: https://www.veracrypt.fr/en/Home.html

If you're really paranoid, you can use the hidden system that will decrypt a dummy drive if someone forces you to give up the password, and some other stuff, but, for now, just use the whole disk encryption. It's a lifesaver.

1. Download Veracrypt from https://www.veracrypt.fr/en/Downloads.html
2. Run the installer package
3. Select "Install"

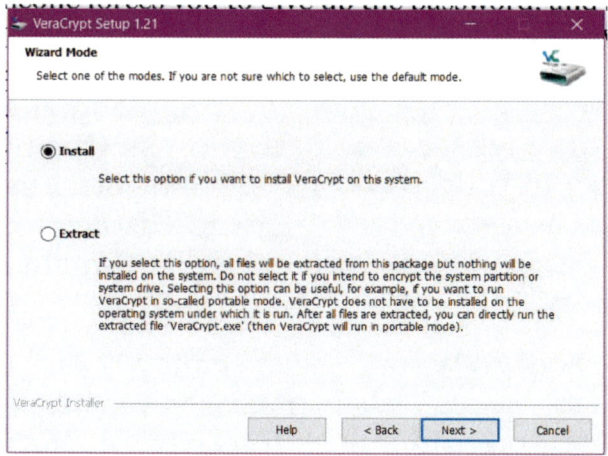

4. Keep the defaults

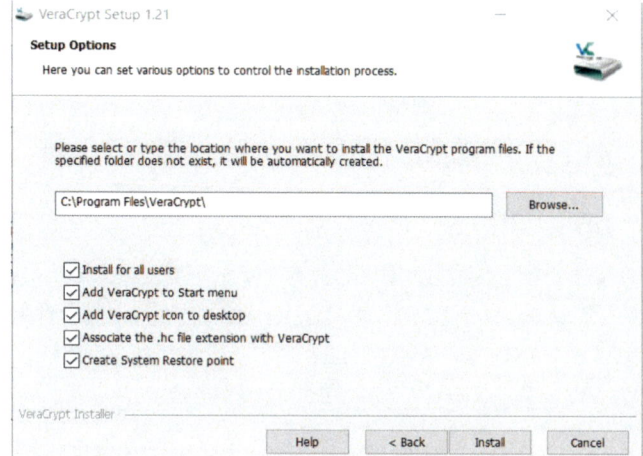

5. Open Veracrypt

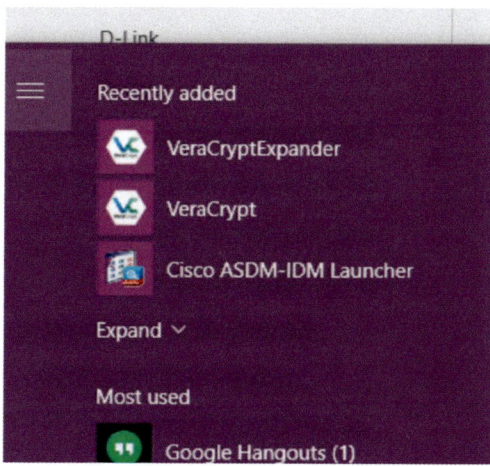

6. Select "Encrypt System Partition / Drive"

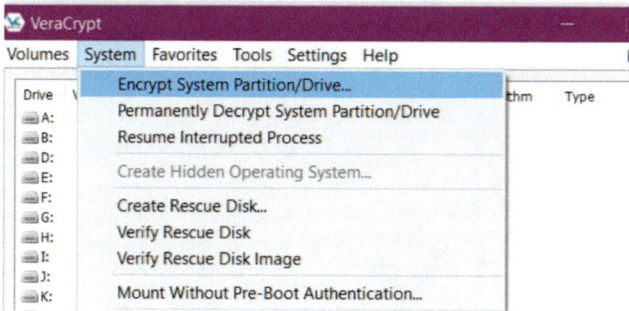

7. Pick an option. If you're paranoid, select "Hidden".

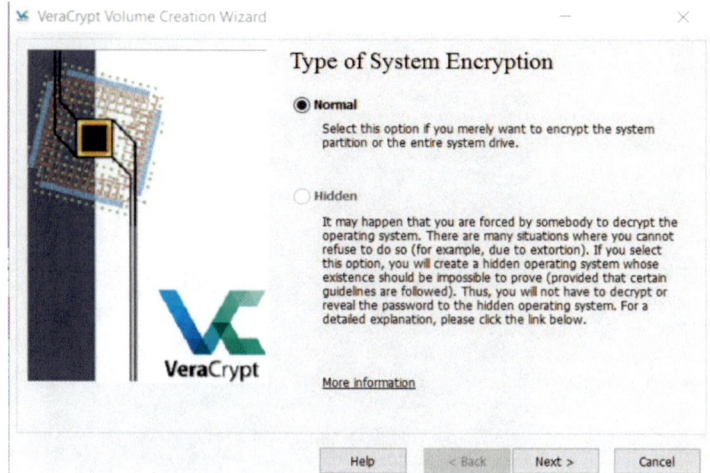

8. Encrypt the system partition

9. You're probably using single-boot

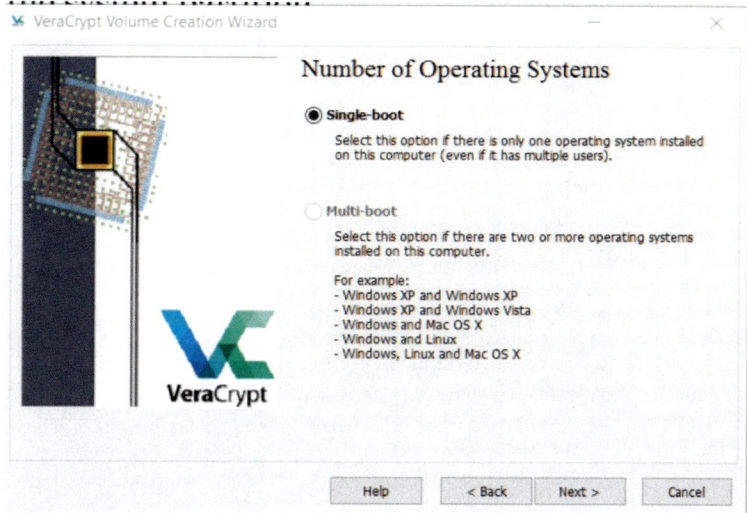

10. Use the defaults

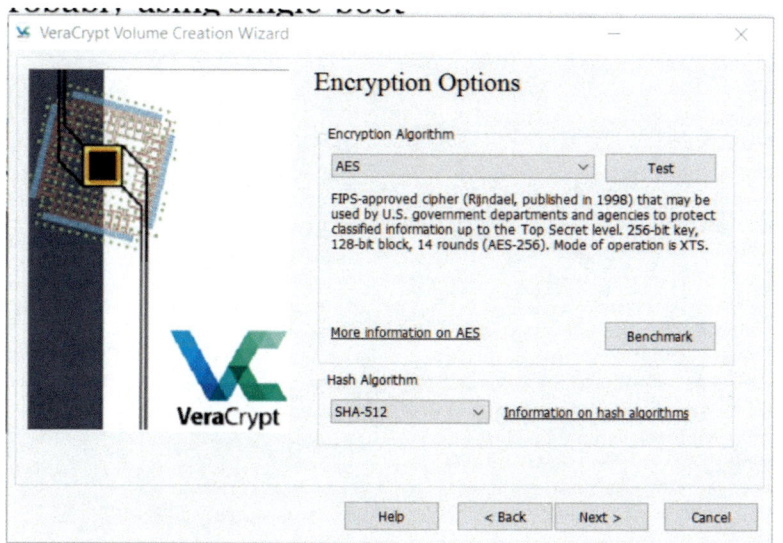

11. Set a password

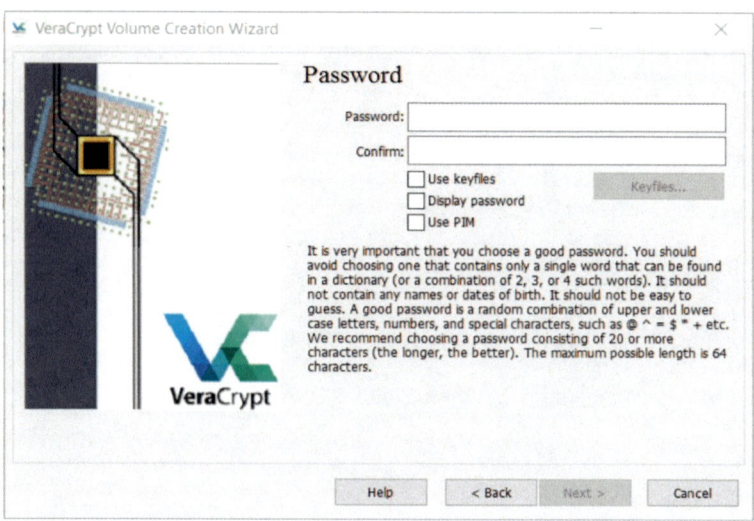

12. Continue following the prompts, using the defaults, until the end. It will encrypt the disk in the background. Let that run overnight.

This way, your hard disk will be encrypted, and nobody without the password will be able to access the data on it, even if they steal your computer.

Final Thoughts

This is, by no means, meant to be everything you can do to secure your computer. There are thousands of security products you can buy and deploy to help prevent breaches. Most information security departments have eighty separate products deployed to manage and monitor their security systems. They hire Managed Security Services Providers to watch the log files. They have dedicated incident response teams to dive on a breach, perform forensic analysis, and shore up the threat vectors. They are able to dedicate diligent, trained people to help keep them secure, and, the sad truth is, there's no such thing as a company which hasn't been breached, there are only companies who don't know they've been breached. Nothing you do will make you one-hundred-percent secure.

That's not to say that this is not worth the effort to make it difficult for them. The concept of low-hanging fruit works to the benefit of the defender as well as the attacker. If you make yourself a hardened target, the average attacker will move on to an easier victim. The steps in this guide will take you a long way toward not being a statistic in the news.

Appendix A: Firewall Ports and Protocols

- tcp/80 (http)
- tcp/443 (https)
- udp/53 (DNS – and it should only be allowed out to 208.67.222.222 and 208.67.220.220, but don't make that change until after you configure OpenDNS)
- udp/123 (Network time protocol)
- tcp/20 and 21 (FTP. Ugh. If ever there were a protocol which should die.)
- tcp/22 (SSH - good stuff)
- tcp/25 (SMTP – used for sending email)
- tcp/465 (Authenticated SMTP)
- tcp/587 (Email Submission protocol)
- tcp/110 (POP3 – for some mail clients)
- tcp/995 (POP3 over SSL)
- tcp/143 (IMAP, for other mail clients)
- tcp/220 (IMAP v3)
- tcp/993 (IMAP over SSL)
- tcp/1723 (PPTP - no, really, there's lots of IoT devices that use that)
- IP/50 (Encapsulated Security Payload for VPN's)
- IP/51 (Authentication Header, for VPN's)

Those should get you started. **FULL DISCLOSURE:** The only reason I use egress filtering anymore is to stop my kids from playing Counterstrike on school nights. It used to be useful to keep malware from calling home to its command and control channels. (C2) Modern malware just uses the ports that it knows will be open. So, yes, you can do that, but you won't really get much out of it. However, since I work for the world's leading manufacturer of firewalls, it would look bad if I didn't cover that at least a bit.

Glossary

- *2-Factor Authentication* – Using two (or more) separate identifying mechanisms to ensure that access is only granted to the correct person. Most commonly used with a password (something you know) and a token (something you have).

- *Address* – Every computer has an address on the network. There are two types of Internet address: IPv4 and IPv6. You're not using IPv6, so your computer will have an address like 192.168.0.2. No, I'm not magic, there's a solid reason why I guessed it correctly, and neither of us wants me to write it out.

- *Attacker* - Any threat actor (bad guy) using malicious methods to separate you from your resources. Those resources could be your money, your data, control over your machine, or even stealing your electricity for their own ends.

- *Browser-* The program you use to surf the Web. You're hopefully using Google Chrome, but I'll (grudgingly) accept Firefox or Opera. **DO NOT USE INTERNET EXPLORER OR MICROSOFT EDGE.** They suck.

- *DNS* – The directory services of the Internet, which maps the names of computers (like www.amazon.com) to IP addresses.

- *Egress Filtering* – Blocking certain ports and protocols outbound to decrease your threat surface

- *Encryption* – Taking plain text (like what you're reading) and using a code, like spies do, to make it unreadable unless you have the specific cipher key to decrypt it.

- *Endpoint* - the actual PC (or smartphone) that you use. You're looking at an endpoint right now. Endpoints connect to other endpoints through the network.

- *Firewall* - A type of network device that acts as a filter between your network and the Big Bad World. Think of it like the badge reader at your office. Nobody (in theory) can enter the building without scanning their badge and being granted access. This is the first line of defense, but one of the weakest.

- *Internet* - Where all the networks converge. We'll have lots of analogies for it later. For right now, think of it as the worst neighborhood in Compton, and you're wandering around with a fat stack of cash hanging out of your pocket, a gold watch, and a Map of the Stars in your hand, marking you as a clueless tourist.

- *Internet Service Provider* – The folks to whom you pay money every month to give you Internet access to your house.

- *Malware* - Any form of virus (spreads using human intervention, like "click on this attachment", Trojan horse (a program that looks useful, like a game, but is really malicious code), worm (spreads without human interaction), rootkit (persistence and evasion mechanism), etc., which is designed to give an attacker control over your system against your will.

- *Network* - the series of routers, switches, wireless access points, cables, cellular towers, satellites, and other media, most of which you will not control, which route data from where it lives to where you want it.

- *Router* - A device that transmits data from one network to another. Your cable provider or DSL provider gave you a (look, nerds, I know, but please remember that this guide is for your mom, not for you) router. Your router may have a couple of antennae on it for your wireless connection. It may not. (I hope they're separate, because if they aren't, you probably don't control your wireless.)

- *Security* - The practice of keeping your stuff safe from the bad guys.

- *Switch* - A kind of hub (I know, but do you really want to explain collision domains to your mom? Me, either.) into which you plug in several Ethernet cables (the ones that look like phone connectors but with 8 pins instead of 4) so that multiple machines can talk to each other.

- *Threat Surface* – The area exposed to attackers. The smaller the threat surface, the harder you are to "hit".

- *User* - You.

- *Wireless Access Point (WAP)* - The thing with antennae that you use to get WiFi to your laptop, phone, smart TV, Internet-enabled sex toy, etc.

Made in the USA
Coppell, TX
06 December 2021

67326140R00040